The Caring Counselor's Book of Reproducibles

More than 100 lively, professional-quality printables for children (PK-5), school staff, and parents

* Worksheets
* Bookmarks
* Coupons
* Games
* Forms
* Handouts
& More

by Maryann Hudgins, LPC

youth light inc.

© 2005 by YouthLight, Inc.
Chapin, SC 29036

Graphic Design and Layout by Amy Rule

ISBN
1889636878

Library of Congress Number
2004115155

Printed in the United States

About the Author

Maryann Hudgins, LPC is the Lead Elementary Counselor for the Grand Prairie Independent School District in Texas. With a Bachelor's degree in Education from Bowling Green State University, a Master degree in Counseling from the University of North Texas, a special education counselor certificate, and a small private practice, she also keeps busy with her service organization affiliations. Maryann has 30 years experience in education, 25 of which have been devoted to the counseling profession. She is a highly sought after motivational speaker and workshop leader.

Acknowledgements

I would like to thank Susan Sharp, my educational role model, for the many years of support and encouragement. She has always gone the extra mile to show that hard work does pay and that in the end, the kids are what matters! I'd be remiss if I didn't mention the wonderful counselors that I have been privileged to work with over the years. These peers are always willing to share ideas and encourage my creativity on a daily basis. The staff of Dickinson Elementary has been my family for over twenty years and continue to nurture and teach the students every day. I also want to thank Connie for her interest in my health. Last, but not least, is the recognition of my cherished family... loving husband, James and talented son, J.P.

Dedication

I dedicate this book to children - who are Today's Pride and Tomorrow's Promise.

-Maryann Hudgins

Table of Contents

Section 1: Affirmations for Children

Section 2: Cards and Notes for Children

Section 3: Guidance Goodies for Children

Section 4: Informational Handouts for Children

Section 5: Affirmations for School Staff and Parents

Section 6: Cards and Notes for School Staff and Parents

Section 7: Guidance Goodies for School Staff and Parents

Section 8: Informational Handouts for School Staff and Parents

Introduction

Sharing ideas has always been a rule of the counseling profession! If something works with one client, chances are that many more individuals will benefit from the same idea. This book includes a variety of reproducible items such as cards, bookmarks, coupons, and games that can be given to children and adults as motivations, incentives or prizes. Our jobs are so busy, isn't it nice to have resources ready at your fingertips?

The many projects included in this book are easily reproducible and can be shared in sessions which could use a little creative edge. This entire collection of lively, professional quality printables can help you avoid "reinventing the wheel" and give your developmental guidance program the boost it may need.

- Maryann Hudgins, LPC

Section I:
Affirmations for Children

This section includes bookmarks, messages in a bottle, fun activities, and more created for children in grades Pre-K through the fifth grade.

Today I will be the best me I can be!

WHY DO YOU THINK THAT PENCILS HAVE ERASERS?

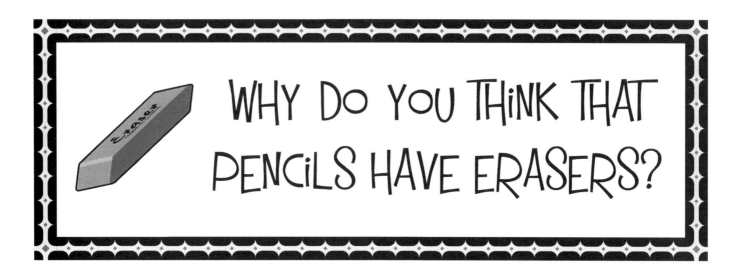

I am responsible for the quality of my work!

Look where you are going!

Education
is not
received ...

Education
is
achieved!

You hold the keys
to your future!

Experience is the best teacher!

Those who bring sunshine into our lives

Cannot keep it from themselves!

My friend is not perfect – nor am I – and so we suit each other admirably.

IF YOU WANT TO GET ALONG, GO ALONG!

Nothing is so strong as gentleness;

Nothing is so gentle as real strength!

Everyone needs their own spot!

Be careful what you wish for...
You just might get it!

If anything is worth doing, it's worth doing right!

It is better to BURN OUT than to RUST!

GOAL *Our greatest glory consists not in never falling, but in rising every time we fall!*

Well done is better than well said.

THE MIND, LIKE A PARACHUTE, FUNCTIONS ONLY WHEN OPEN!

Cut out these labels and wrap them around bottles. Fill the bottles with the messages on the following two pages.

Children are not fooled. They know we give time to the things we love!

The best time for you to hold your tongue is when you feel you must say something or burst.

A person's wealth is no greater than the worth of his ambitions.

Quarrels would not last long if the fault was only on one side!

Kindness can be its own motive. We are made kind by being kind.

If you really want to be happy, nobody can stop you!

Good humor is one of the best articles of dress one can wear in society.

The mighty oak was once just a little nut that held its ground!

The tongue must be heavy indeed, since so few people can hold it!

The time that you enjoy wasting is not wasted!

A true friend always knows the right thing to say... even when it is nothing.

It is better to give than to receive... especially advice!

Genius is one percent inspiration and ninety-nine percent perspiration.

Better by far that you should forget to smile
than that you remember and be sad.

Always do right. This will gratify some people and astonish the rest.

There is no better time than now to be happy.
Happiness is a journey not a destination.

Friendships multiply joys and divide grief.

To find joy in another's joy; that is the true secret of happiness.

It is not enough to have great qualities; one must make good use of them!

The best things happen to those who make the best of things that happen!

Speak when you are angry, and you'll make the best speech you'll ever regret!

Advice is what we ask for when we already know the answer but wish we didn't!

Level with children... no one spots a phony quicker than a child!

Children need strength to lean on, a shoulder to cry on,
And an example to learn from.

How to Make a Paper "Me Box"

Make your box out of any cardstock or paper you find that contains a theme that you are trying to emphasize. You can also tear off the front of old greeting cards and paste them to decorate these boxes. Or, have a child draw pictures or paste magazine images on each side of the box to tell about him/herself.

Measure from corner to corner of the piece of paper to find its center.

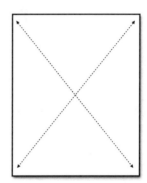

Figure 1

Fold each of the four sides into the middle of the paper, making a good crease and then opening the paper back up to full-size.

Figure 2

Cut the long sides of the paper to where the folds intersect creating flaps A-D. Fold the four flaps up and in towards the center creating sides 3 and 4. Fold the longer edges of sides 1 and 2 over the flaps to complete the box.

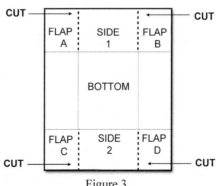

Figure 3

Enlarge and print on 8½" x 14" paper. Add buttons in place of missing "O's".

G   d friends
are like
unique
butt   ns...
XXXXXXXXXX
Y   u c   llect
them   ne
at a time.

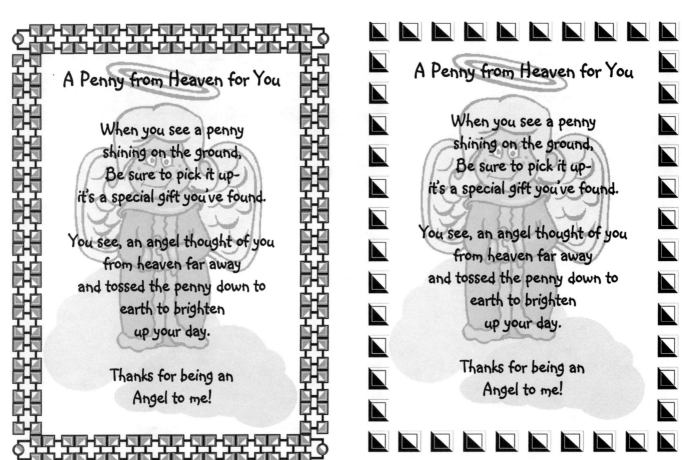

A Penny from Heaven for You

When you see a penny
shining on the ground,
Be sure to pick it up-
it's a special gift you've found.

You see, an angel thought of you
from heaven far away
and tossed the penny down to
earth to brighten
up your day.

Thanks for being an
Angel to me!

A Penny from Heaven for You

When you see a penny
shining on the ground,
Be sure to pick it up-
it's a special gift you've found.

You see, an angel thought of you
from heaven far away
and tossed the penny down to
earth to brighten
up your day.

Thanks for being an
Angel to me!

You can duplicate this sheet on cardstock and attach a penny to each poem to give as keepsakes.

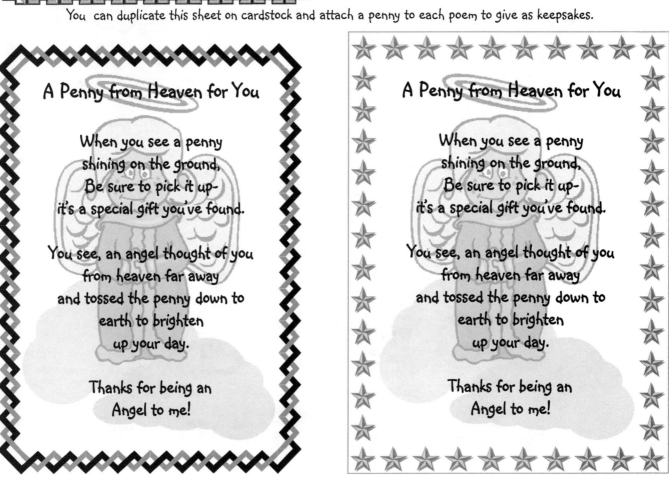

A Penny from Heaven for You

When you see a penny
shining on the ground,
Be sure to pick it up-
it's a special gift you've found.

You see, an angel thought of you
from heaven far away
and tossed the penny down to
earth to brighten
up your day.

Thanks for being an
Angel to me!

A Penny from Heaven for You

When you see a penny
shining on the ground,
Be sure to pick it up-
it's a special gift you've found.

You see, an angel thought of you
from heaven far away
and tossed the penny down to
earth to brighten
up your day.

Thanks for being an
Angel to me!

Dreams do come true...

Draw yourself as a success in the future.

If I work at it hard enough I can... _____

_____

_____

_____

_____

Section 2: Cards and Notes for Children

This section includes coupons to share, ID cards, and more created for children in grades Pre-K through the fifth grade.

Special Gift Certificate

TO: _____

FOR: _____

Date: _____

Authorized Signature

Expiration Date:

Just for you!

Special Gift Certificate

TO: _____

FOR: _____

Date: _____

Authorized Signature

Expiration Date:

Just for you!

Special Gift Certificate

TO: _____

FOR: _____

Date: _____

Authorized Signature

Expiration Date:

Just for you!

Special Gift Certificate

TO: _____

FOR: _____

Date: _____

Authorized Signature

Expiration Date:

Just for you!

Special Gift Certificate

TO: _____

FOR: _____

Date: _____

Authorized Signature

Expiration Date:

Just for you!

Special Gift Certificate

TO: _____

FOR: _____

Date: _____

Authorized Signature

Expiration Date:

Just for you!

Telephone Safety Numbers

NAME	NUMBER

Name: _____

I'm in the _____ grade.

Teacher's Name:
_____

Favorite Subject:
_____

My Hobbies:
_____

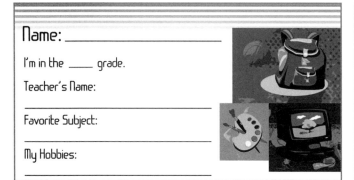

Name: _____

I'm in the _____ grade.

Teacher's Name:
_____

Favorite Subject:
_____

My Hobbies:
_____

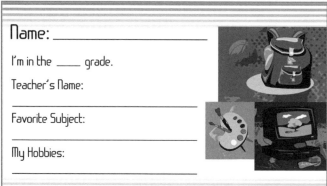

Name: _____

I'm in the _____ grade.

Teacher's Name:
_____

Favorite Subject:
_____

My Hobbies:
_____

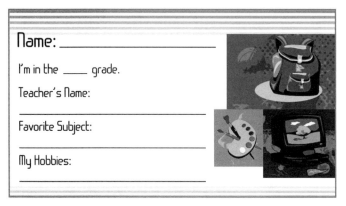

Name: _____

I'm in the _____ grade.

Teacher's Name:
_____

Favorite Subject:
_____

My Hobbies:
_____

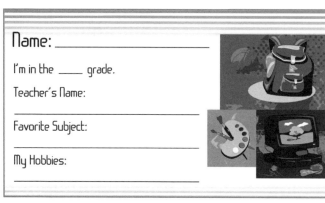

Name: _____

I'm in the _____ grade.

Teacher's Name:
_____

Favorite Subject:
_____

My Hobbies:
_____

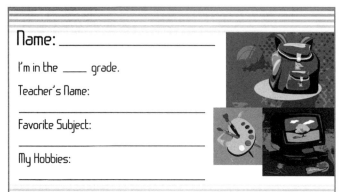

Name: _____

I'm in the _____ grade.

Teacher's Name:
_____

Favorite Subject:
_____

My Hobbies:
_____

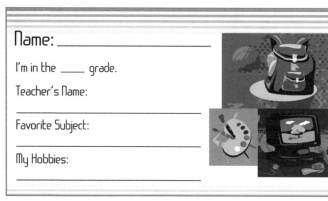

Name: _____

I'm in the _____ grade.

Teacher's Name:
_____

Favorite Subject:
_____

My Hobbies:
_____

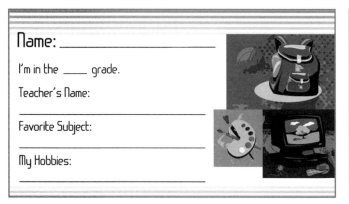

Name: _____

I'm in the _____ grade.

Teacher's Name:
_____

Favorite Subject:
_____

My Hobbies:
_____

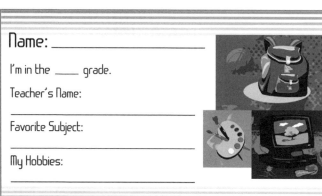

Section 3:
Guidance Goodies
for Children

This section includes passes, worksheets, games, activities, and more created for children in grades Pre-K through the fifth grade.

HALL PASS

STUDENT: _____

TEACHER: _____

TIME: _____ DATE: _____

Restroom　　　Office　　　Counselor

Cafeteria　　　Library　　　Other

Special Classes　　Computer Lab

HALL PASS

STUDENT: _____

TEACHER: _____

TIME: _____ DATE: _____

Restroom　　　Office　　　Counselor

Cafeteria　　　Library　　　Other

Special Classes　　Computer Lab

HALL PASS

STUDENT: _____

TEACHER: _____

TIME: _____ DATE: _____

Restroom　　　Office　　　Counselor

Cafeteria　　　Library　　　Other

Special Classes　　Computer Lab

Late Pass

Student:_____

Date:_____ Time:_____

Reason:

- ☐ Overslept
- ☐ Running Late
- ☐ Sick
- ☐ Car Trouble
- ☐ Dentist Appt.
- ☐ Doctor Appt.
- ☐ Other

_____
Signature

Late Pass

Student:_____

Date:_____ Time:_____

Reason:

- ☐ Overslept
- ☐ Running Late
- ☐ Sick
- ☐ Car Trouble
- ☐ Dentist Appt.
- ☐ Doctor Appt.
- ☐ Other

_____
Signature

Late Pass

Student:_____

Date:_____ Time:_____

Reason:

- ☐ Overslept
- ☐ Running Late
- ☐ Sick
- ☐ Car Trouble
- ☐ Dentist Appt.
- ☐ Doctor Appt.
- ☐ Other

_____
Signature

Late Pass

Student:_____

Date:_____ Time:_____

Reason:

- ☐ Overslept
- ☐ Running Late
- ☐ Sick
- ☐ Car Trouble
- ☐ Dentist Appt.
- ☐ Doctor Appt.
- ☐ Other

_____
Signature

Name _____ **Date** _____

Daily Behavior Chart

	On Task	Positive Behavior	Complete Work
Morning Activities			
Reading			
Math			
Lunch			
P.E. / Music			
Science / Social Studies			
Language			
Hallways/Restroom			

1 = Poor   2 = Fair   3 = Good   4 = Great
Teacher Initials = Unacceptable

COMMENTS:

STUDENT IS RESPONSIBLE TO HAVE THE TEACHER COMPLETE THIS FORM BEFORE CLASSES END.

_____
Parent Signature

HOW DO YOU FIND AND KEEP A FRIEND?

In each box below, write about or draw yourself doing what it says.

GIVE COMPLIMENTS

ASK QUESTIONS ABOUT THEM

OFFER TO HELP

LISTEN TO WHAT THEY SAY

HERO VS. HERO GAME

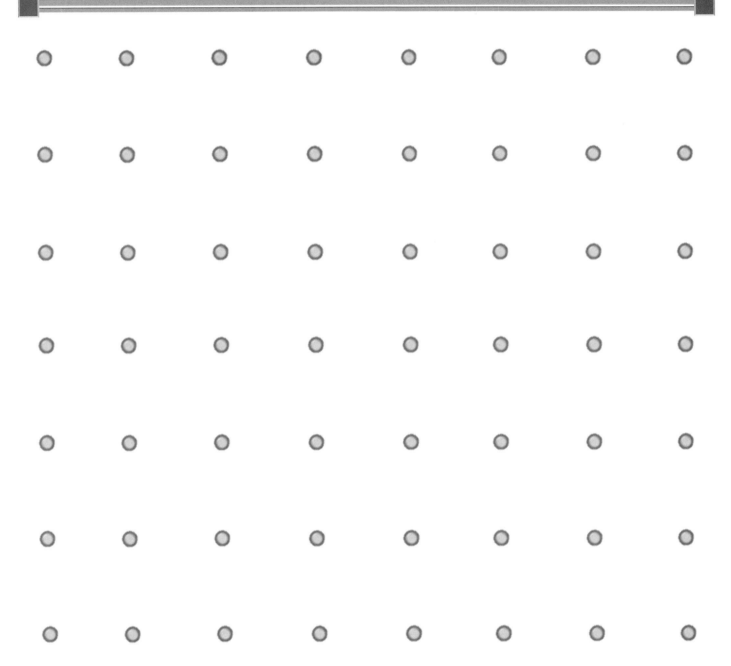

TWO TO FOUR PLAYERS. EACH PERSON TAKES A TURN PUTTING A LINE FROM ONE DOT TO ANOTHER DOT. IF YOU ARE THE PERSON TO MAKE A BOX OUT OF FOUR DOTS, YOU CAN PUT THE INITIALS OF YOUR HERO INSIDE THE BOX! WINNER HAS THE MOST BOXES AT THE END!

Golden Rule

Do unto others as you would have them do unto you.

Aristotle
We should behave to others as we wish others behave to us.

Buddhism
Hurt not others with that which pains thyself.

Christianity
Do unto others as you would have them do unto you.

Confucius
What you do not want done to yourself, do not do unto others.

Hinduism
Do nothing to thy neighbor which thou wouldst not have him do unto thee thereafter.

Islam
No one of you is a believer unless he loves for his brother what he loves for himself.

Judaism
What you dislike for yourself, do not do to anyone.

Respect

Session One

Name: _____ Date: _____

1. If I am crying, I'd like someone to _____
_____

2. If someone is angry, I'd like them to _____
_____

3. If I have extra money, I'd like to be able to _____
_____

4. If I know the answer to a question in class, I'd like _____
_____

5. If my friend is sad, I would _____
_____

6. If I am chosen last in a game, I would want _____
_____

Respect
Session Two

Ages	Jobs
Skin Tones	Activities

This activity will be a small group project. Each table of four students will have a supply of magazines to cut out pictures. The pictures will be placed under the headers on 9"x 12" construction paper to show the vast differences in people.

After the posters are complete the students can share their findings with the class. It is very important that we see differences in a positive light... we learn to accept and respect the things that are familiar to us. The more we are exposed to differences, the sooner we can learn to appreciate others in their uniqueness!

Ages

Jobs

Skin Tones

Activities

Respect

Session Three

Discuss the situations and work on solutions to the problems by brainstorming.

A) Joe is in the third grade and he has one sister in kindergarten and one sister in the fifth grade. Every morning seems to be a problem for Joe because he has a hard time taking a shower before breakfast. His sisters take forever to fix their hair in the bathroom! If he gets upset and yells at them, he gets in trouble with Mom. What might be some other ways that Joe can solve his situation?

B) Shawna wants to go to the roller rink on Thursday evening with the other girl scouts. Shawna has a chore chart that she is responsible for every afternoon after school.

> Monday - Vacuum living room
> Tuesday - Empty dishwasher
> Wednesday - Fold and put away clean clothes
> Thursday - Empty bathroom trash cans
> Friday - Water the plants in the sunroom

She also has to study for her spelling test that she will take on Friday. Today is Tuesday. Is there any way that Shawna might be able to do all these things if she plans her week carefully? What do you think she could do?

C) Steven learned a new way to disagree respectfully. His Mom told him to remember the word ACTS whenever he runs into a situation that is troubling for him.

> A - Always look at both sides
> C - Calmly explain your views
> T - Take time to listen to the other person
> S - Solve your disagreement

Steven's best friend wants to go to the old abandoned house after school today. He thinks this might be dangerous because he heard that the floors are rotting away. Can you figure out how to help Steven talk to his friend? Try to use the ACTS method!

Respect
Session Four

| Who's in Charge? | How Can You Show Respect? (circle your answer) |

Who's in Charge?

How Can You Show Respect?
(circle your answer)

1. Teacher

A. Finish your homework
B. Turn in paper without a name

2. Police Officer

A. Cross in crosswalk
B. Don't wear seatbelt

3. Parent

A. Whine about bedtime
B. Help with chores

4. Bus Driver

A. Sit and talk quietly
B. Throw trash on the floor

5. Babysitter

A. Hide and scare them
B. Help pick up toys

6. Doctor

A. Scream "No shots!"
B. Take your medicine

7. Coach

A. Run laps
B. Make excuses to sit out

8. Grandparent

A. Make them a "Thank You" card
B. Beg for a toy at the store

9. Scout Leader

A. Get jealous when someone wins
B. Help another scout earn a badge

10. Movie Theater Usher

A. Sit down in your seat
B. Throw popcorn

Responsibility
Session One

Healthy Habits	Unhealthy Habits
Brush Teeth	Eat Lots of Candy
Wear Clean Clothes	Tear Up Your New Shoes
Make Your Bed	Turn in Sloppy Work
Wash Your Hair	Interrupt People
Take a Bath/Shower	Argue
Eat Fruits and Vegetables	Break Toys
Be Helpful	Complain About Chores
Smile	Whine
Be a Good Listener	Throw Clothes on the Floor

When does someone praise you? _____

_____

How does that feel? _____

_____

What do you do that makes you feel proud? _____

_____

What habit do you need to build? _____

_____

Which bad habit do you need to stop? _____

_____

Responsibility
Session Two

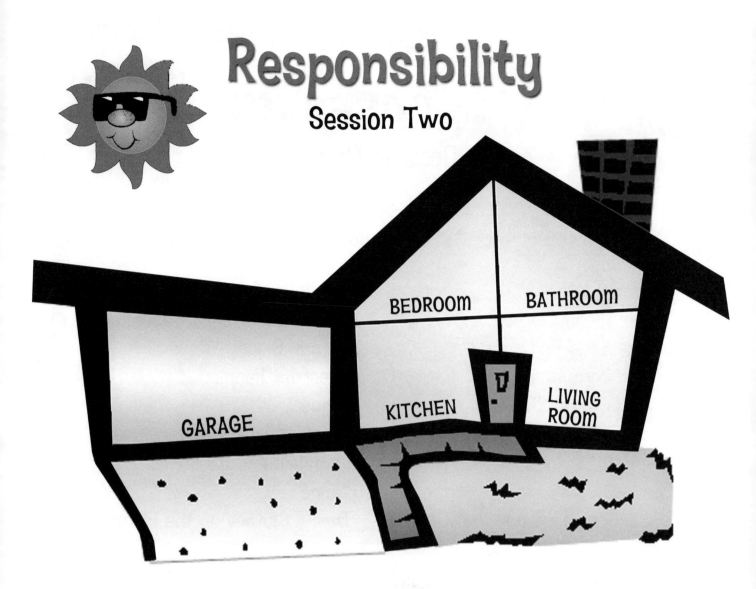

BEDROOM

BATHROOM

KITCHEN

LIVING ROOM

GARAGE

CHORES

Put the letter in the correct area of the house. Some letters go in several areas of the house.

A) Hang up towels

B) Pick up clothes

C) Pull weeds

D) Turn off lights

E) Rinse off dishes

F) Make bed

G) Share TV time

H) Pick up toys

I) Put away bike

J) Eat dinner

K) Vacuum

L) Dust furniture

Responsibility

Session Three

Fill in the missing letters to find responsible school behaviors!

Li_ten   to   the   _each_r

Wal_   q_iet_y   in   the   ha_ls

Do   yo_r   be_t   on   pa_ers

B_ing   all   y_ur   s_pp_ies

Rai_e   yo_r   ha_ds

Kno_   the   r_les

Fin_sh   w_rk   ne_tly

Stu_y   for   t_sts

Fo_low   d_re_tions

Ta_e   tur_s

Letters to use

d s e u w n

u t l r e o

u l l k n l

c a s p s u

a t u l l o

l a k u

Responsibility

Session Three

In a group, brainstorm examples of how different activities are age appropriate. For example, a twelve year old can take their own shower or bath but not a five year old. Five year olds can help clear the table after dinner but not clean the dishes. Talk it over!

Younger Children	Older Children
1._____	1._____
_____	_____
2._____	2._____
_____	_____
3._____	3._____
_____	_____
4._____	4._____
_____	_____
5._____	5._____
_____	_____
6._____	6._____
_____	_____
7._____	7._____
_____	_____
8._____	8._____
_____	_____

MY SPECIAL MOMENT IN TIME

This is a picture of the
MOST EXCITING DAY
in my life.
Ask me about it!

Name: _____

Name: _____

WE ARE NOT PERFECT...
NOT EVEN CLOSE, SOMETIMES!

Circle the words that express how you feel when things go wrong!

Nervous

Guilty

Calm

Scared

Angry

SAD

HAPPY

UPSET

EXCITED

Embarrassed

Name: _____

Color My Feelings

If colors were feelings, make each balloon the color you think the feeling would look like.

Happy

Sad

Angry

Scared

Kind

Name: _____

My Vocabulary of Feelings

Using the word bank, place the feelings in the correct columns.

👍 Pleasant	Unpleasant 👎
1.	1.
2.	2.
3.	3.
4.	4.
5.	5.
6.	6.
7.	7.
8.	8.
9.	9.

WORD BANK

Scared	Angry	Truthful
Bored	Brave	Determined
Lonely	Patient	Furious
Tired	Anxious	Happy
Excited	Calm	Frustrated
Gentle	Doubtful	Sincere

Name: _____

FeeLiNgs CoLLaGe

In the space below, find and paste pictures from old magazines that show different feelings!

Name: _____

Amazing Acrostics

Use the word down the center of each box to build other words that describe it. The first one is done for you!

Box 1:

```
            F  U  N  N  Y
    F R I E N D L Y
  B R A V E
  G U I L T Y
  W O R R I E D
        A N G R Y
        G R E A T
    U P S E T
```

Center word (vertical): F E E L I N G S

Box 2:

Center word (vertical): R E S P E C T F U L

Box 3:

Center word (vertical): R E S P O N S I B L E

Box 4:

Center word (vertical): C I T I Z E N S H I P

44

Name: _____

Ingredients For a
Good Friendship

Circle the ingredients necessary for a good friendship.

Fun

Selfish

Kind

Mean

Calm

Nice

Trust

Bossy

SPECIAL CODES

Have fun solving the coded messages and writing your own messages in code!

_ _ _   _ _ _ _ _ _ _ _   _ _ _   _ _ _ _ .

_ _ _ _ _ _ _ _ _ _   _ _   _ _ _ _   _ _ _ _ .

_ _ _   _ _ _   _ _ _ _ _   _ _ _   _ _ _ _ _ _ .

_ _ _ _ _   _ _ _ _   _ _ _ _ _ _ _ _   _ _ _ _ .

_ _ _   _ _   _ _ _   _ _ _ _   _ _ _ _ _ ?

A	B	C	D	E	F	G	H	I	J	K	L	M
↳	⇷	⇇	⇆	↕	⇶	⇵	⇇	⇉	↑↑	↓↓	∩	∪

N	O	P	Q	R	S	T	U	V	W	X	Y	Z
↱	↰	∪	∪	↺	⊼	^	⌐	_	_	⇧	⇧	⇦

Name: _____

Name:_____

SHINING STARS

Everyone has stars that twinkle...
Write in the words that show your
good qualities.

PATIENT   **FORGIVING**   **ACCEPTING**

CARING   **RELIABLE**   **HELPFUL**

HONEST   **RESPECTFUL**   **CONFIDENT**

Name: _____

ANGER
(One Tough Feeling)

The following is a relaxation technique for you to use when you begin to DEAL with this feeling.

1. Sit Comfortably

2. Close Your Eyes

3. Think About Your Breathing

4. Count Each Deep Breath in to 10.

5. Blow Out the Air Through Your Mouth

6. Repeat 10 Times

7. Think About a Peaceful Time for You

8. Ask Yourself What You Need to Do

9. Talk Over Your Solution With Someone

10. Get Ready to Let Go of Any Negative Thoughts

STOP... Breathe... Count to 10

48

Name: _____

Upset Feelings

John woke up late and was having a hard time getting to school on time. He had to get a late pass and serve detention after school. He said, "That's great!" What did he really feel?

Kesha found out that she is getting glasses for the first time. She hopes that the kids won't make fun of her. She really wants to be able to see the board better. She said, "Who cares!" How might she be feeling?

Larry was going to present his book report in front of the class. He loved this book and wanted everyone else to read it, too. Just before his turn, Larry saw that Beth was standing to discuss the same book! "Now what?" What should he do?

Jen liked to sit with Maryann at the lunch table. They had been best friends for years. Today they have a new rule in the lunchroom. They have to sit alphabetically! "That's wrong!" said Susie. What is something she can do?

Special Sayings

Each day of our lives we make deposits in the memory banks of our children.

-Charles R. Swindoll

Think for yourself and let others enjoy the privilege of doing so too.

-Voltaire

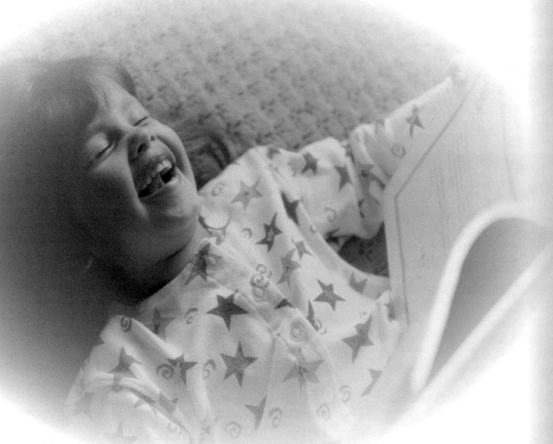

Sticks and stones are hard on bones
Aimed with angry art,
Words can sting like anything
But silence breaks the heart.

-Suzanne Nichols

We need 4 hugs a day for survival.
We need 8 hugs a day for maintenance.
We need 12 hugs a day for growth.

-Virginia Satir

Interview of Friends

1. What is your full name?

2. Who lives at your house?

3. What is your favorite subject?

4. Tell me something that makes you proud.

5. If you could be anyone else... Who would you be?

6. What would you like to do for a job when you grow up?

7. Tell me what you like to do on Saturday.

8. If you could make one wish, what would it be?

Take some time to talk with your friend and then share the new information that you learned with others! That's what a reporter always does!

Interview of Family

1. Who do you look most like?

2. Who do you think has the hardest job in a family?

3. What is your favorite chore around the house?

4. What should happen when someone breaks a rule at home?

5. If you won a million dollars, what would you do?

6. Which schools did you go to?

7. Tell me what you like to do on Saturday.

8. If you could make one wish, what would it be?

Take some time to talk with your family and then share the new information that you learned with others! That's what a reporter always does!

Interview of a School Staff Person

1. What is your full name?

2. What is the name of your job?

3. How long have you been at this school?

4. What do you do in your job?

5. Did you have to go to school after you graduated to work in this job?

5. Did you always want to do this job? What else did you think of doing?

7. Tell me what you like to do on Saturday.

8. If you could make one wish, what would it be?

Take some time to talk with this person and then share the new information that you learned with others! That's what a reporter always does!

Section 4:
Informational
Handouts
for Children

This section includes informational handouts on subjects such as grief, anger management, test taking and more created for children in grades Pre-K through the fifth grade.

GRIEF & LOSS: It's all about CHANGE

Things that change

Hair grows	Leaves fall from trees
New baby	Move away from friends
Someone dies	New job for Dad
Get married	Start school in new grade
Parents divorce	Sister goes to college

Everyone experiences things that change everyday. Some of the things are exciting and fun and some of them are sad or scary. Change is all around us and we have to learn to cope with new situations. Some helpful ideas that you can use would be:

- ☆ Talk to someone you trust.
- ☆ Read a book to get more information.
- ☆ Do fun things that you like to do.
- ☆ Know that your feelings are okay.
- ☆ Ask for help.

*Why do things change? The best answer may be "just because." Sometimes we have no way of coming up with an answer ... We just have to go on with our days and try to make the best out of a tough situation. It might help to know that **everyone** needs to find a way to handle these situations ... Even grown ups!*

Ten things to do instead of staying
ANGRY!

* Take a walk

* Play with clay

* Read a book

* Listen to music

* Draw or paint

* Help a friend

* Do some exercises

* Talk with someone

* Watch a special movie

* Write a funny story

What to do???
Conflict Resolution

Tips to Try

Walk away from trouble.

Try to ignore the person or situation.

Laugh and answer in a friendly way.

Confront the person and ask what is happening.

Listen to the problem.

State your views.

Use a calm, normal voice.

Tell what you expect to have happen.

Stay in control - count to ten.

Talk to an adult if you can't come to an understanding.

TACKLING TESTS

METHODS FOR STUDYING AND TESTING

READ

Read over the information you are suppose to know. It can be the book, your notes from the teacher, study guides, worksheets, or anything that will help you to learn and remember the information.

THINK ABOUT IT

Figure out the major points. What are the ideas, dates, people, or skills that you are trying to remember in the chapter or unit that you studied.

ORGANIZE

How does the information fit together? List the key points or make an outline showing the most important information. Now you can fill in the details that you remember under each point.

PRACTICE

Figure out if you need to *see it, say it,* or *do something* to get the ideas to stay with you ... Sometimes it takes a little of each method! Don't forget to ask for help when you need to figure out the best way to successfully study! Sometimes having a study buddy makes all the difference!

TIPS FOR TESTING DAYS

REST THE NIGHT BEFORE	BE ON TIME
EAT A GOOD BREAKFAST	DRESS COMFORTABLY
REMAIN CALM	CHECK YOUR ANSWERS

UNDERSTANDING GROWN UPS

(Surprise yourself & them)

What you always wanted to know ...

☺ Grown ups were kids once ... may be even now!

☺ Grown ups like to have some personal alone time.

☺ Grown ups make mistakes every single day.

☺ Grown ups have feelings, too.

☺ Grown ups have many different responsibilities.

☺ Grown ups need reminders of our love for them.

☺ Grown ups aren't perfect - no one is!

☺ Grown ups are responsible for their own happiness.

☺ Grown up problems, like divorce, are theirs to figure out on their own.

Remember

Children often feel like they need to make the adults in their lives satisfied and happy. The BEST way to do this is to work on your own thoughts and actions first!

True Leaders are Seen & Heard

Here are a few questions that will help you identify leaders ... see if you can recognize anyone you know!

- ✓ Who would you ask for help in your class?
- ✓ Who can you look to to help you make a decision?
- ✓ Who can get kids to work together in a group without hurting someone's feelings?
- ✓ Who can be comfortable with grown ups and kids?
- ✓ Who would you ask to help you if you were sad or hurt?
- ✓ Who is chosen as the team captain in games?
- ✓ Who seems to understand things that others have a hard time figuring out?
- ✓ Who likes to help others settle their differences?
- ✓ Who seems to show a lot of self control and confidence?

Leaders are people that have a sense of knowing what needs to be done and how to do it in the best way! Some people have a natural ability and others work hard to show these qualities. If you are wanting to show more leadership qualities, you might want to work on some of the following ideas.

- ❑ Help others to cooperatively work together.
- ❑ Ask to help someone in need.
- ❑ Get others excited about projects.
- ❑ Organize others to get things done.
- ❑ Listen to the ideas that others have.
- ❑ Be fair with ALL situations & include everyone in projects.
- ❑ Have a sense of humor and fair play!

Section 5:
Affirmations for
School Staff
and Parents

This section includes bookmarks, messages in a bottle, magnet sheet, candy wrappers and more created for school staff and parents.

 It amazes me how cheerful, how optimistic you can be in this crazy world of ours. You don't know what's going on either, do you?

No matter how serious your life requires you to be, everyone needs a friend to act goofy with!

Remember that each door you open... Each life you enter... Deserves special care!

Let no day end before you have spoken words of love, friendship, and thanks!

"Children need strength to lean on, a shoulder to cry on, and an example to learn from."

Advice is what we ask for when we already know the answer but wish we didn't.

I'd rather have a mind opened by wonder... Than closed by belief!

Level with children...

No one spots a phony quicker than a child.

If we give our children one thing... let it be enthusiasm!

The only person who ever got all their work done by Friday was Robinson Crusoe.

Kindness is the sunshine that grows friendship!

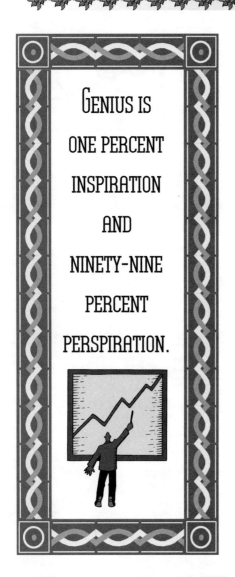

GENIUS IS ONE PERCENT INSPIRATION AND NINETY-NINE PERCENT PERSPIRATION.

Better by far that you should forget and Smile than that you should remember and be Sad.

Be patient with everyone, but above all with yourself.

Always do right. This will gratify some people and astonish the rest.

Quarrels would not last long if the fault was only on one side!

Good Nature

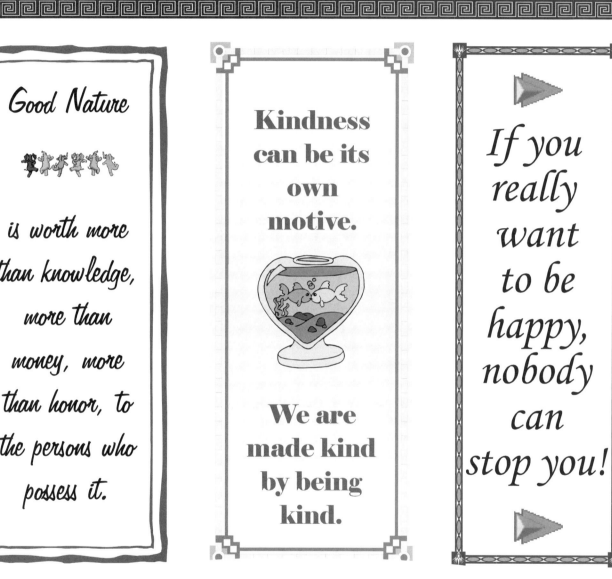

is worth more than knowledge, more than money, more than honor, to the persons who possess it.

Kindness can be its own motive.

We are made kind by being kind.

If you really want to be happy, nobody can stop you!

Good humor is one of the best articles of dress one can wear in society.

A skeptic is a person who when he sees the handwriting on the wall, claims it's forgery!

Sorrow looks back, worry looks around, and faith looks up...

The best way to get even is to forget...

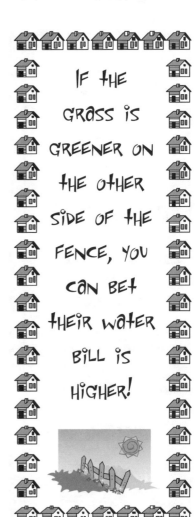

IF THE GRASS IS GREENER ON THE OTHER SIDE OF THE FENCE, YOU CAN BET THEIR WATER BILL IS HIGHER!

Keep smiling, and...
If you see someone's missing one...
Give them one of yours!

It's not as bad a world as some would make it; but whether it's good or bad depends on how you take it!

You have not lived until you have done something for someone who can never repay you!

Have a nice day... unless, of course, you've already made other plans!

You may be only one person in the world... But you may be the world to one person !

The best way to get the last word... is to apologize!

Cut out these labels and wrap them around bottles. Fill the bottles with the messages on the following two pages.

Children are not fooled. They know we give time to the things we love!

The best time for you to hold your tongue is when you
feel you must say something or burst.

A person's wealth is no greater than the worth of his ambitions.

Quarrels would not last long if the fault was only on one side!

Kindness can be its own motive. We are made kind by being kind.

If you really want to be happy, nobody can stop you!

Good humor is one of the best articles of dress one can wear in society.

The mighty oak was once just a little nut that held its ground!

The tongue must be heavy indeed, since so few people can hold it!

The time that you enjoy wasting is not wasted!

A true friend always knows the right thing to say...
even when it is nothing.

It is better to give than to receive... especially advice!

Genius is one percent inspiration and ninety-nine percent perspiration.

Better by far that you should forget to smile
than that you remember and be sad.

Always do right. This will gratify some people and astonish the rest.

There is no better time, than now, to be happy.
Happiness is a journey not a destination.

Friendships multiply joys and divide grief.

To find joy in another's joy; that is the true secret of happiness.

It is not enough to have great qualities; one must make good use of them!

The best things happen to those who make the best of things that happen!

Speak when you are angry, and you'll make the best speech you'll ever regret!

Advice is what we ask for when we already know the answer but wish we didn't!

Level with children... no one spots a phony quicker than a child!

Children need strength to lean on, a shoulder to cry on,
and an example to learn from.

BE MODERATE IN ALL THINGS...

Especially moderation!

A Woman...
Has to do twice as much as a man
to be considered half as good.
Fortunately, this isn't difficult!

Practice random acts of intelligence & senseless acts of self-control!

WEL.COM

THIS ONLY LOOKS LIKE A DESK...

It's actually a large trash can with drawers and four legs!

Many things are opened by mistake...but none so often as the mouth!

THE BUCK DOESN'T EVEN SLOW DOWN HERE!

Laminate and attach a magnet on the back for great gifts!

Special Jar of Love

If I could capture all my love
this, I tell you, I would do.
I'd put it in a keepsake bottle
Made especially for you!

You'd never, ever have to be blue,
'Cause you'd have plenty love
to last all the year through!

So, here is a special bottle,
Though all my love won't fit.
I still stuffed tons of hugs and kisses
Down inside of it!

Every time that you feel down or sad, just remember this
bottle of love! You can take hugs & kisses out any time
you need to - and they'll never run out!

72

SEEDS OF WISDOM

SEEDS OF WISDOM

SEEDS OF WISDOM

You will need: Snack size baggies, beans, peas, popcorn kernels, or large flower seeds

This simple idea works well as a reminder that we all need to start at the beginning in order to grow and accomplish our ideas and dreams. Place several seeds in the baggie and staple the "Seeds of Wisdom" label on the top. What a fun way to ease the stress at test time with this vote of confidence!

I found a penny today
Just lying on the ground,
But it's not just a penny
This little coin I've found.

Found pennies come from heaven
That's what my Grandpa told me,
He said angels toss them down
Oh, how I loved that story.

He said when an angel misses you
They toss a penny down,
Sometimes just to cheer you up
To make a smile out of a frown.

So don't pass by that penny
When you're feeling blue,
It may be a penny from heaven
That an angel tossed to you!

You can duplicate this sheet on cardstock and attach a penny to each poem to give as keepsakes.

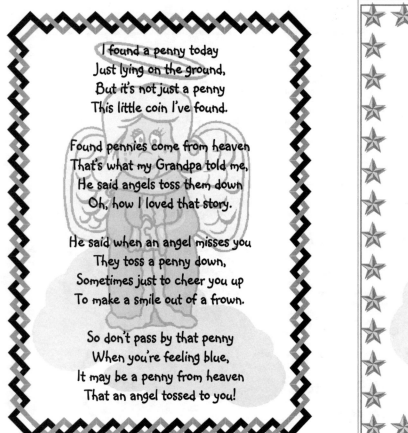

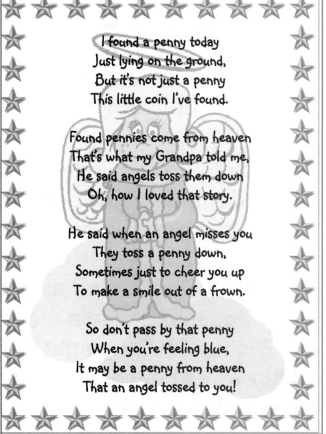

Candy Wrappers

Cut out the candy wrapper on this page and fold it around a full-size chocolate bar. Cut out the wrappers on the next page and fold them around miniature chocolate bars. Use tape or glue to fasten.

Lifelong Ingredients:
Laughs, Friends, Smiles, Rest, Good Times, and Memories

Elementary

Counselors Care

Children are our Future!
Today's Pride & Tomorrow's Promise

Nutrition Facts
Serving Size:
1 Special Person

Amt/Serving	% DV
Rest	100%
Recreation	100%
Relaxation	100%

Life Long
Ingredients:

Laughs,
Friends, Smiles, Fun,
Good Times & Memories.

 Elementary
**Counselors
Care**

Children are our future!

Life Long
Ingredients:

Laughs,
Friends, Smiles, Fun,
Good Times & Memories.

Elementary
**Counselors
Care**

Children are our future!

Life Long
Ingredients:

Laughs,
Friends, Smiles, Fun,
Good Times & Memories.

Elementary
**Counselors
Care**

Children are our future!

Life Long
Ingredients:

Laughs,
Friends, Smiles, Fun,
Good Times & Memories.

 Elementary
**Counselors
Care**

Children are our future!

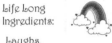
Life Long
Ingredients:

Laughs,
Friends, Smiles, Fun,
Good Times & Memories.

 Elementary
**Counselors
Care**

Children are our future!

Life Long
Ingredients:

Laughs,
Friends, Smiles, Fun,
Good Times & Memories.

 Elementary
**Counselors
Care**

Children are our future!

Life Long
Ingredients:

Laughs,
Friends, Smiles, Fun,
Good Times & Memories.

 Elementary
**Counselors
Care**

Children are our future!

Life Long
Ingredients:

Laughs,
Friends, Smiles, Fun,
Good Times & Memories.

 Elementary
**Counselors
Care**

Children are our future!

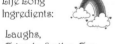
Life Long
Ingredients:

Laughs,
Friends, Smiles, Fun,
Good Times & Memories.

 Elementary
**Counselors
Care**

Children are our future!

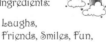
Life Long
Ingredients:

Laughs,
Friends, Smiles, Fun,
Good Times & Memories.

 Elementary
**Counselors
Care**

Children are our future!

Life Long
Ingredients:

Laughs,
Friends, Smiles, Fun,
Good Times & Memories.

 Elementary
**Counselors
Care**

Children are our future!

Life Long
Ingredients:

Laughs,
Friends, Smiles, Fun,
Good Times & Memories.

 Elementary
**Counselors
Care**

Children are our future!

Section 6:
Cards and Notes
for School Staff
and Parents

This section includes desk notes, character coupons, and more created for school staff and parents.

HOT NEWS!

From: _____   Date: _____

_____

_____

_____

_____

_____

CAN YOU HELP ME FIND MY WAY?

FROM: _____   DATE: _____

_____

_____

_____

_____

I am not disorganized...

I have anti-systematic methodology disorder!

From: _____ Date: _____

_____

_____

_____

_____

No Lion...
I need you to know...

From: _____ Date: _____

_____

_____

_____

_____

Character Certificate

To: _____   From: _____

Pillar Shown: _____

For the following: _____

Date: _____

_____
Authorized Signature

Character Certificate

To: _____   From: _____

Pillar Shown: _____

For the following: _____

Date: _____

_____
Authorized Signature

Character Certificate

To: _____   From: _____

Pillar Shown: _____

For the following: _____

Date: _____

_____
Authorized Signature

Counselor's Care Cards

Use these as business cards or however you like!

Counselors' Care

Counselors' Care

Counselors' Care

Counselors' Care

Counselors' Care

Counselors' Care

Counselors' Care

Counselors' Care

Elementary School Counselor Cards

Fill these out as business cards or use them however you wish.

Elementary School Counselor

Elementary School Counselor

Elementary School Counselor

Elementary School Counselor

Elementary School Counselor

Elementary School Counselor

Elementary School Counselor

Elementary School Counselor

Section 7:
Guidance Goodies
for School Staff
and Parents

This section includes guidance forms, games, signs, a collection of motivations, and more created for school staff and parents.

RECORD OF CONTACT

Date	Child's Name	Grade/ Teacher	Comments	Parent	Parent Meeting	Refer

Weekly Guidance

Week of: _____

	Monday	Tuesday	Wednesday	Thursday	Friday
8:30-9:00					
9:00-9:30					
9:30-10:00					
10:00-10:30					
10:30-11:00					
11:00-11:30					
11:30-12:00					
12:00-12:30					
12:30-1:00					
1:00-1:30					
1:30-2:00					
2:00-2:30					
2:30-3:00					

Always subject to change by you or me as needed!

DAILY CONTRACT

If I get _____ check marks today, I will get to

visit _____ in the morning for a

special treat!

GOALS -----
8:00 - 8:30
8:30 - 9:00
9:00 - 9:30
9:30 - 10:00
10:00 - 10:30
10:30 - 11:00
11:00 - 11:30
11:30 - 12:00
12:30 - 1:00
1:00 - 1:30
1:30 - 2:00
2:30 - 3:00
3:00 - 3:30

Acceptable _____   Comments:

Unacceptable _____   _____

Signature

Behavior Contract

I, _____ , agree to improve my behavior and attitude. I know and understand the rules and expectations of my campus and agree to take the responsibility for my actions to achieve academic success. Some of the specific plans for quality behavior that I have are:

1. _____

_____

2. _____

_____

3. _____

_____

4. _____

_____

5. _____

_____

Behavior Plan

Answer the questions below. Your answers will create an outline for your final full page essay.

1. What was I doing? _____

_____

_____

2. How was my behavior inappropriate (wrong)? _____

_____

_____

3. What do I want to do now? _____

_____

_____

4. What could be the best way of getting what I want? _____

_____

_____

5. What will I do when I've completed my plan? _____

_____

_____

6. How can I make my plan work? _____

_____

_____

Situational Plan

WHAT happened? _____

_____

WHERE did it happen? _____

HOW did it happen? _____

_____

WHO was involved? _____

_____

WHEN did it happen? _____

WHY did it happen? _____

_____

Now you are ready to discuss this with an adult!

Testing

Please
Do not
Disturb

TESTING

Please

Do Not Disturb

(Shh!)

Communication

This form can be used to brainstorm the many ways in which we communicate. Fill in the blanks to complete a whole world of communication styles!

Physical	Senses	Emotions	Art Form	Objects	Technology	Written	Thoughts	Verbal

Communication

ANSWER KEY

Physical	Senses	Emotions	Art Form	Objects	Technology	Written	Thoughts	Verbal
Gestures	Hearing	Tears	Song	Light Beam	TV / Radio	Magazines	Dreams	Words
Expressions	Touch	Laughs	Dance	Mirror	Radar	Newspaper	Feelings	Tone of Voice
Actions	Taste	Anger	Music	Smoke Signals	Fax	Books	Spoken	Pitch
	Smell		Visual Art		Sonar	Drawings	Silent	Speed
	Sight				Telephone	Symbols		Volume
					Morse Code	Letters		Inflection
					Satellite			
					Computer			
					Internet			

Twenty-One Lessons To Live By

1. Give people more than they expect and do it cheerfully.

2. Marry a man / woman you love to talk to. As you get older, their conversational skills will be as important as any other.

3. Don't believe all you hear, spend all you have, or sleep all you want.

4. When you say, "I love you," mean it.

5. When you say, "I'm sorry," look the person in the eye.

6. Be engaged at least six months before you get married.

7. Believe in love at first sight.

8. Never laugh at anyone's dreams. People who don't have dreams don't have much.

9. Love deeply and passionately. You might get hurt but it's the only way to live life completely.

10. In disagreements, fight fairly. No name calling.

11. Don't judge people by their relatives.

12. *Talk slowly but think quickly.*

13. *When someone asks you a question you don't want to answer, smile and ask, "Why do you want to know?"*

14. *Remember that great love and great achievements involve great risk.*

15. *Say "bless you" when you hear someone sneeze.*

16. *When you lose, don't lose the lesson.*

17. *Remember the three R's: Respect for self; Respect for others; and responsibility for all your actions.*

18. *Don't let a little dispute injure a great friendship.*

19. *When you realize you've made a mistake, take immediate steps to correct it.*

20. *Smile when picking up the phone. The caller will hear it in your voice.*

21. *Spend some time alone.*

A true friend is someone who reaches for your hand, and touches your heart.

The Starfish Flinger

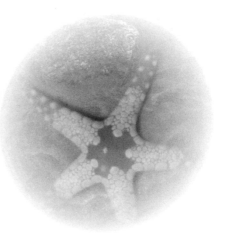

As the old man walked down the beach at dawn, he noticed a young man ahead of him picking up starfish and flinging them into the sea. Finally catching up with the youth, he asked him why he was doing this. The answer was that the stranded starfish would die if left until the morning sun. "But the beach goes on for miles. There are millions of starfish. How can your effort make a difference?" The young man looked at the starfish in his hand and then threw it to the safety of the sea. "It makes a difference to this one." he said.

-Author Unknown

The Starfish Flinger

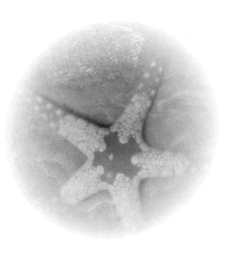

As the old man walked down the beach at dawn, he noticed a young man ahead of him picking up starfish and flinging them into the sea. Finally catching up with the youth, he asked him why he was doing this. The answer was that the stranded starfish would die if left until the morning sun. "But the beach goes on for miles. There are millions of starfish. How can your effort make a difference?" The young man looked at the starfish in his hand and then threw it to the safety of the sea. "It makes a difference to this one." he said.

-Author Unknown

The Starfish Flinger

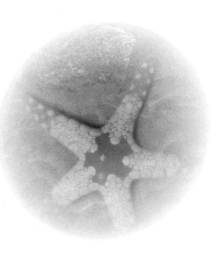

As the old man walked down the beach at dawn, he noticed a young man ahead of him picking up starfish and flinging them into the sea. Finally catching up with the youth, he asked him why he was doing this. The answer was that the stranded starfish would die if left until the morning sun. "But the beach goes on for miles. There are millions of starfish. How can your effort make a difference?" The young man looked at the starfish in his hand and then threw it to the safety of the sea. "It makes a difference to this one." he said.

-Author Unknown

The Sense of a Goose

When you see geese flying along in "V" formation, you might consider what science has discovered as to why they fly that way. As each bird flaps its wings, it creates an uplift for the bird immediately following. By flying in "V" formation, the whole flock adds at least 71 percent greater flying range than if each bird flew on its own.

People who share a common direction and sense of community can get where they are going more quickly and easily because they are traveling on the thrust of one another.

When a goose falls out of formation, it suddenly feels the drag of trying to go it alone - and quickly gets back into formation to take advantage of the lifting power of the bird in front.

If we have as much sense as a goose, we will stay in formation with those people who are headed the same way we are.

When the head goose gets tired, it rotates back in the wing and another goose flies point.

It is sensible to take turns doing demanding jobs, whether with people or with geese flying south.

Geese honk from behind to encourage those up front to keep up their speed.

What messages do we give when we honk from behind?

Finally - and this is important - when a goose gets sick or is wounded by gunshot, and falls out of formation, two other geese fall out with that goose and follow it down to lend help and protection. They stay with the fallen goose until it is able to fly or until it dies, and only then do they launch out on their own, or with another formation to catch up with their group.

If we have the sense of a goose, we will stand by each other like that.

By Source Unknown

Maya Angelou was interviewed by Oprah one day. She really is a marvel who has led quite an interesting and exciting life. She was asked by Oprah what she thought of growing older and there on television, she said it was exciting. There were so many things occurring everyday to marvel at... like her breasts. They seem to be in a race for her waist... and one day, one would be in the lead and another day, it would be the other in the lead. The entire audience laughed so hard they cried. She is such a simple and honest woman... with so much wisdom in her words. Because of that, I share this...

 # Food for thought...

I've learned that you can tell a lot about a person by the way he/she handles these three things: a rainy day, lost luggage, and tangled Christmas tree lights.

I've learned that regardless of your relationship with your parents, you'll miss them when they are gone from your life.

I've learned that making a "living" is not the same thing as making a "life."

I've learned that life sometimes gives you a second chance.

I've learned that you shouldn't go through life with a catcher's mitt on both hands. You need to be able to throw something back.

I've learned that whenever I decide something with an open heart, I usually make the right decision.

I've learned that even when I have pains, I don't have to be one.

I've learned that every day you should reach out and touch someone.

I've learned that people love a warm hug, or just a friendly pat on the back.

I've learned that I still have a lot to learn.

I've learned that people will forget what you said, people will forget what you did, but people will never forget how you made them feel.

By Maya Angelou

TODAY

I woke up early today, excited over all I get to do before the clock strikes midnight. I have responsibilities to fulfill today. My job is to choose what kind of day I am going to have.

Today I can complain because the weather is rainy or I can be thankful that the grass is getting watered for free.

Today I can feel sad that I don't have more money or I can be glad that my finances encourage me to pay my purchases wisely and guide me away from waste.

Today I can grumble about my health or I can rejoice that I am alive.

Today I can lament over all that my parents didn't give me when I was growing up or I can be grateful that they allowed me to be born.

Today I can mourn my lack of friends or I can excitedly embark upon a quest of being friendly.

Today I can murmur because I have to do housework or I can feel honored because I have shelter for my mind, body and soul.

Today stretches ahead of me, waiting to be shaped. And here I am the sculptor who gets to do the shaping. What today will be like is up to me. I get to choose what kind of day I will have!

Have a great day... Unless you have other plans!

Eight Gifts that Don't Cost a Thing

1. The gift of Listening...
   But you must REALLY listen. No interrupting, no daydreaming, no planning your response - just listening.

2. The gift of Affection...
   Be generous with appropriate hugs, kisses, pats on the back and handholds. Let these small actions demonstrate the love you have for family and friends.

3. The gift of Laughter...
   Clip cartoons. Share articles and funny stories. Your gift will say, "I love to laugh with you."

4. The gift of a Written Note...
   It can be a simple "Thank you for your help" note or a full sonnet. A brief handwritten note may be remembered for a lifetime and may even change a life.

5. The gift of a Compliment...
   A simple and sincere "You look great in red" "You did a super job" or "That was a wonderful meal" can make someone's day.

6. The gift of a Favor...
   Every day go out of your way to do something kind.

7. The gift of Solitude...
   There are times when we want nothing better than to be left alone. Be sensitive to those times and give that gift to others, too.

8. The gift of a Cheerful Disposition...
   The easiest way to feel good is to extend a kind word to someone. Really, it is not that hard to say "Hello" or "Thank you." Friends are a a very rare jewel, indeed. They make you smile and encourage you to succeed. They lend an ear, they share a word of praise and they open their hearts to us. Show them you care!

100

If I Had My Child to Raise Over Again

If I had my child to raise all over again,

I'd build self esteem first, and the house later.

I'd finger paint more, and point fingers less.

I'd do less correcting and more connecting.

I'd take my eyes off my watch,

and watch with my eyes.

I would care to know less and know to care more.

I'd take more hikes and fly more kites.

I'd stop playing serious, and seriously play.

I would run through more fields

and gaze at more stars.

I'd do more hugging and less tugging.

I'd see the oak tree in the acorn more often.

I'd be firm less often, and affirm much more.

I'd model less about the love of power,

And more about the power of love.

-Diane Loomas

Phone Trick

Strange but it works!!!

Key in the first 3 digits of your phone number (not your area code) into a calculator.

Multiply by 80.

Add 1.

Multiply by 250.

Add the last four digits of your phone number.

Add the last four digits of your phone number again.

Subtract 250.

Divide by 2.

Is it your phone number?

Number Trick

Have you ever wanted to *dazzle* a group with your brilliance? This fun project can have them asking for more! Sometimes it is a great way to allow kids to "put one over" on the adults in their lives!

Have someone fill out the worksheet on the next page and solve the equation without showing you their work. It is fine for them to include all of their extended/step family in the numbers they provide.

When they are done solving the equation, have them give you their grand total. Amaze them by telling them exactly how many brothers, sisters and grandparents they have by their answer.

The number in the hundreds place is the number of brothers they have. The number in the tens place is the number of sisters they have. The number in the ones place is the number of living grandparents they have.

For example, if the answer is 431, then they have 4 brothers, 3 sisters and 1 living grandparent. If the answer is 33, then they have 0 brothers, 3 sisters and 3 living grandparents. If the answer is 2, then they are an only child with two living grandparents.

-Source Unknown

HAVE FUN!

Name: _____ Date: _____

Number Trick Worksheet

_____ **x 2 =** _____
Number of   Total 1
Brothers

_____ **+ 3 =** _____
Total 1   Total 2

_____ **x 5 =** _____
Total 2   Total 3

_____ **+** _____ **=** _____
Total 3   **Number of**   Total 4
           Sisters

_____ **x 10 =** _____
Total 4   Total 5

_____ **+** _____ **=** _____
Total 5   **Number of Living**   Total 6
          Grandparents

_____ **- 150 =** _____
Total 6   **Grand Total**

Sum Of Three Dice

This simple trick leaves the students wondering ... Is this real? Of course, the idea is to share the secret while helping the children pump up their addition and subtraction skills! They will feel so empowered to share this with their families and friends that they will never realize they are working with each roll of the dice.

The object is to predict what the sum of the bottom of three dice will be by counting the dots on the top of the dice and then subtracting that number from 21. A roll of three, six and four will result in an answer of eight, which is the sum of the numbers that lay against the table (five, one and two). To arrive at your answer, simply add the top numbers (3+6+4=13) and then subtract that answer from 21 (21-13=8). Encourage the children to try doing the math in their head so that they can impress everyone when they are able to predict the sum of the three dice.

Watch the children enjoy this self esteem building project!!!

Section 8:
Informational Handouts
for School Staff
and Parents

This section includes informational handouts on grief, divorce, parenting, and more created for school staff and parents.

What does grief look like... for us and the kids?

Stage 1
We are in a state of shock.

Stage 2
We express emotions.

Stage 3
We feel depressed and lonely.

Stage 4
We may have physical symptoms of distress.

Stage 5
We may feel a sense of guilt about the loss.

Stage 6
We may feel anger or resentment.

Stage 7
Gradually hope comes through.

Stage 8
We struggle to affirm reality.

Parenting Gifts For Children

Parents always want to give their children gifts that money just can't buy! We do this by the ways we react to situations and problems.   Sometimes this can be so rewarding that we can transform their lives by a word, look or touch. What an awesome responsibility we have when raising our children! By our reactions to experiences we offer our children the opportunity to learn how to handle situations ... sometimes even when we make mistakes ... we teach our children the skill of asking for forgiveness! What a lesson that becomes when we show them that we are not perfect.

Childhood in general takes patience from the adults involved. When we say that "Actions speak louder than words," we are opening ourselves to constant watchful eyes. Pretty scary place to be, but so is the child's world. The benefit we get from from living a life of fun and connection is that we experience a joy we can share with others. Being together doing "nothing" can mean more to a child needing acceptance than all the trips to the toy store combined.

CHILDREN MODEL WHAT THEY SEE!

Some symptoms of ADHD are described as inattention, difficulty in performing tasks, hyperactivity and impulsivity.

♦ **Inattention:** Where a person often fails to give close attention to details or makes careless mistakes, often has difficulty sustaining attention in tasks, often does not seem to listen when spoken to directly, or often does not follow through on instructions.

♦ **Tasks:** Where a person often has difficulty organizing tasks and activities, often avoids, dislikes or is reluctant to engage in tasks that require sustained mental effort, often loses things necessary for tasks or activities, is often easily distracted by extraneous stimuli, or is often forgetful in daily activities.

♦ **Hyperactivity:** Where a person often fidgets with hands or feet or squirms in seat, often feels restless, often has difficulty engaging in leisure activities quietly, or often talks excessively.

♦ **Impulsivity:** Where a person often blurts out answers before questions have been completed, or often interrupts or intrudes on others.

ADHD symptoms in infants

♦ Extreme restlessness, crying, poor sleep patterns
♦ Difficult to feed
♦ Constant thirst
♦ Frequent tantrums, head banging and rocks the cot

ADHD symptoms in older children

♦ Poor concentration and brief attention span
♦ Increased activity - always on the go
♦ Impulsive - doesn't stop to think
♦ Fearless and takes undue risks
♦ Poor co-ordination
♦ Weak short term memory
♦ Inflexible personality
♦ Lacks self esteem
♦ Sleep and appetite problems continue
♦ Normal or high IQ but under performs at school

Not all infants and children with ADHD have all the features of the condition and there are different degrees of severity.

DIVORCE
Questions from the kids!

Be prepared ...

- ❑ What does it mean to get a divorce?
- ❑ Why do some parents divorce?
- ❑ Is it ok to talk about the divorce?
- ❑ Is the divorce my fault?
- ❑ Now what happens to our family?
- ❑ How am I suppose to feel?
- ❑ Who's going to take care of me?
- ❑ Will I have two houses?
- ❑ Where will I be on Holidays and Birthdays?
- ❑ What if I miss Mom or Dad?
- ❑ What if I don't miss Mom or Dad?
- ❑ Will I be stuck in the middle?
- ❑ What about my Grandparents?
- ❑ What if I feel like a secret keeper or messenger?
- ❑ Will my parent's ever get back together?
- ❑ What if they date other people?
- ❑ Am I still important?

Dear Parents,

Is your parenting style preparing your child for the twenty-first century?

Are you an *authoritarian* parent?

This parent values obedience. Commanding the child what to do and what not to do, rules are clear and unbending. The parent pours the "right" information into the child who is considered an empty vessel. Misbehavior is strictly punished.

Predominant for most of Western history, authoritarian parenting is effective in societies experiencing little change and accepting one way to do things. The child learns by imitating the expert.

This style mismatches a rapidly changing society which values choice and innovation. Rebellion often results from strict punishment. Spanking, which models violence as a solution to problems, is contradictory in a society which claims to value peaceful solutions. And children raised to follow the "expert" easily copy anyone, including undesirable peers.

Are you a *permissive* parent?

Popular in the 1950's and 60's, this style was a reaction to the horrors of whole nations following the dictators in Word War II. Instead of following, children are encouraged to think for themselves, avoid inhibitions, and not value conformity. Parents take a "hands-off" approach, allowing children to learn from the consequences of their actions. Misbehavior is usually ignored.

Although those raised in this style are creative and original, they often have trouble living in a highly populated community as well as fitting into the work-force. Ignoring misbehavior gives no information about expected behavior. With no intervention, the bully wins, while the passive child loses, a perfect set-up to be a victim in later life. Aggressive patterns become ingrained when children are not guided to find acceptable ways to get desires met.

Unlike the child-oriented 50's and 60's where one consistent adult was available to patiently guide self-discovery to the consequences of actions, today's society is fast-paced with a multitude of adults playing into the child's life each week. Without clear limits, children get confused, feel insecure, and can make poor choices.

Are you an *assertive-democratic* parent?

These parents establish basic guidelines for children. Clarifying issues, they give reasons for limits. Learning to take responsibility is a high priority. Children are given lots of practice in making choices and guided to see the consequences of those choices. Misbehavior is handled with an appropriate consequence or by problem-solving with the child to find an acceptable way to get desires met. Out-of-control children have "cool-off" time, not punishment. Children are part of deciding how to make amends when someone or something has been hurt. Assertive-democratic parenting is the best for today's fast-changing information age where choice is constant and there is no longer just one "right" way. Children raised by this style learn to accept responsibility, make wiser choices, cope with change, and are better equipped to succeed in a work-force which relies on cooperative problem-solving.

Parenting is the hardest job you will ever have ... but the MOST rewarding in life. It is a learning process everyday and one that's message reflects that

Children are Today's Pride & Tomorrow's Promise!

What can I say in a crisis situation ... and be helpful?

Empathy and Rapport

- I am so sorry that this happened to you.
- This must be a very difficult time for you right now.
- I can hear / see that you are having a hard time with this.
- You don't have to handle this on your own.

Identification

- What I hear you saying is....
- Do you think it would be helpful if we talked about how you felt at the time.
- How do you think you reacted at that time?
- I know that it may not be easy to do, but can we talk about this some more.

Validation

- It sounds like you are angry right now.
- You did not do anything wrong.
- What you are feeling is not uncommon.